Program Authors

Peter Afflerbach

Camille Blachowicz

Candy Dawson Boyd

Elena Izquierdo

Connie Juel

Edward Kame'enui

Donald Leu

Jeanne R. Paratore

P. David Pearson

Sam Sebesta

Deborah Simmons

Susan Watts Taffe

Alfred Tatum

Sharon Vaughn

Karen Kring Wixson

SAVVAS
LEARNING COMPANY

We dedicate Reading Street to
Peter Jovanovich.

His wisdom, courage,
and passion for education
are an inspiration to us all.

RENAISSANCE
Accelerated Reader

ISBN-13: 978-0-328-72438-3
ISBN-10: 0-328-72438-6

21   20

Dear Reader,

What do you think of Reading Street so far? You've learned lots of letters and sounds and words. Have AlphaBuddy and your *My Skills Buddy* helped you along the way?

On the next part of our trip, you will read about plants and animals, and there will be a special visit to a very large beanstalk.

So hop on board, and let's get going. There's lots more to learn.

Sincerely,
The Authors

Look at Us!

How are animals and plants unique?

Flowers
Big Book

Week 2

Big Book

Nonfiction • Science
Nature Spy by Shelley Rotner and Ken Kreisler

Unit 2 Contents

Week 5

Week 6

Don Leu
The Internet Guy

Right before our eyes, the nature of reading and learning is changing. The Internet and other technologies create new opportunities, new solutions, and new literacies. New reading comprehension skills are required online. They are increasingly important to our students and our society.

Those of us on the Reading Street team are here to help you on this new, and very exciting, journey.

See It!

- **Big Question Video**

- **Concept Talk Video**

- **Envision It! Animations**

- **eReaders**

Hear It!

- *Sing with Me Animations*

- *eSelections*

- **Grammar Jammer**

Adam and Kim **play at the beach.**

Concept Talk Video

File   Edit   View   Favorites   Tools   Help

http://www.ReadingStreet.com

Do It!

- Story Sort

- eReaders

- Letter Tile Drag and Drop

Look at Us!

THE BIG
?

How are animals and plants unique?

Let's Listen for

Initial Sounds

Read Together

- Say *Ann, Al, Andy.* What sound do you hear at the beginning of these names?

- Find three things that begin with /a/, like *Ann.*

- Point to these pictures and say these words: *bed, pillow, rug.* Do they begin with the same sound? What about *ant, alligator, astronaut?*

- What rhymes with *Ann?*

READING STREET ONLINE
BIG QUESTION VIDEO
www.ReadingStreet.com

© **Common Core State Standards**

Informational Text 3. With prompting and support, describe the connection between two individuals, events, ideas, or pieces of information in a text.

Comprehension

Envision It!

Compare and Contrast

READING STREET ONLINE
ENVISION IT! ANIMATIONS
www.ReadingStreet.com

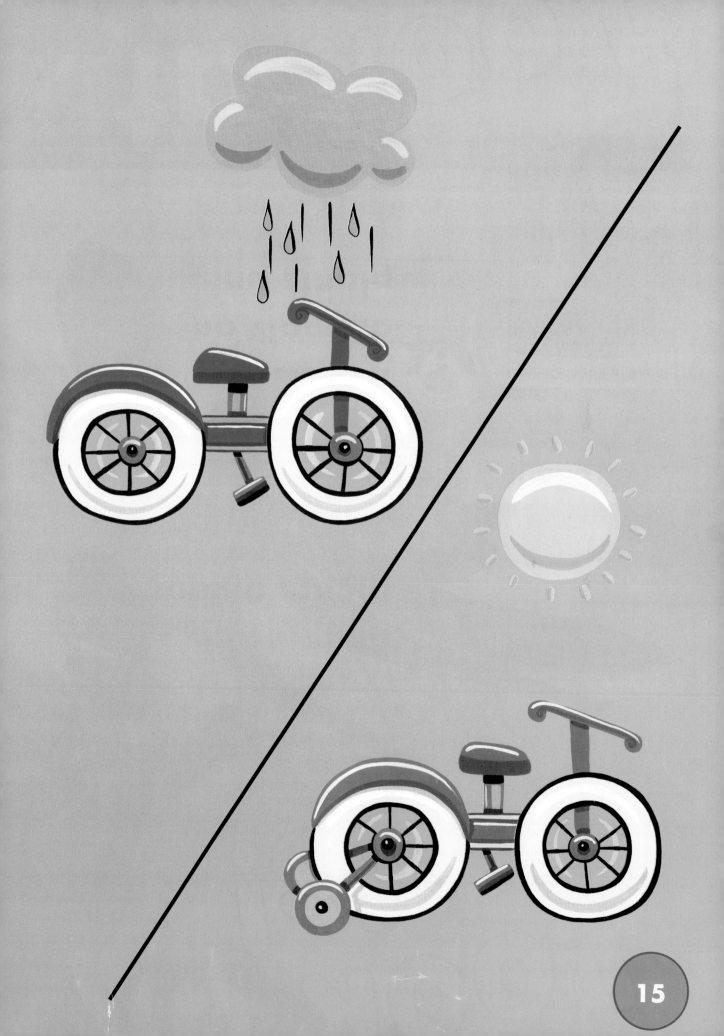

Aa

astronaut

READING STREET ONLINE
ALPHABET CARDS
www.ReadingStreet.com

Phonics

Short Aa

Words I Can Blend

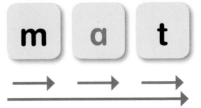

m a t

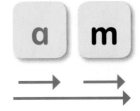

a m

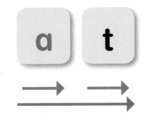

a t

T a m

Words I Can Read

have

is

Sentences I Can Read

1. I have a mat.
2. The mat is little.
3. Tam is little.

Common Core State Standards
Foundational Skills 4. Read emergent-reader texts with purpose and understanding.
Also Foundational Skills 3., 3.a., 3.c.

Phonics

I Can Read!

Decodable Reader

- Short *a*
  am
  Tam
  mat
  at

- High-Frequency Words
  I
  am
  is
  little
  have
  a
  the

▲ Read the story.

A Little Mat

Written by Alex Altman
Illustrated by Mary Stern

Decodable Reader 7

I am Tam.

Is Tam little?

Tam is little.

I have a mat.

Is the mat little?

The mat is little.

Tam is at the mat.

Common Core State Standards
Informational Text 1. With prompting and support, ask and answer questions about key details in a text. **Also Informational Text 2.**

Envision It! | Retell

Flowers
by Vijaya Khisty Bodach
Gail Saunders-Smith, PhD, Consulting Editor

Big Book

**READING STREET ONLINE
STORY SORT**
www.ReadingStreet.com

26

Think, Talk, and Write

1. Tell about a unique flower you have seen. Text to Self

2. How are a rose and a cauliflower alike? How are they different?

↻ Compare and Contrast

3. Look back and write.

Let's

It!

Vocabulary

- ● What do you see that is yellow?

- ■ What do you see that is purple?

- ▲ What do you see that is orange?

Listening and Speaking

- ● What happens first in the story?

- ■ What happens next in the story?

- ▲ What happens last in the story?

Vocabulary

Color Words

yellow

purple

orange

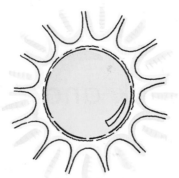

Listen for Sequence

Be a good listener!

Common Core State Standards
Literature 1. With prompting and support, ask and answer questions about key details in a text. **Also Literature 2., 5., 9.**

Let's Practice It!

Fable

- Listen to the fable.

- How are the two characters different?

- What is the field like in summer? in winter?

- How is this story like "The Boy Who Cried Wolf!"?

- What new expression does this fable teach you?

The Ant and the Grasshopper

1

Common Core State Standards
Foundational Skills 2.d. Isolate and pronounce the initial, medial vowel, and final sounds (phonemes) in three-phoneme (consonant-vowel-consonant, or CVC) words. **Also Foundational Skills 2.a., 2.e.**

Phonemic Awareness

Let's Listen for

Initial Sounds

Read Together

● Say *Sam, Seth, Sue.* What sound do you hear at the beginning of these names?

■ Point to the sun. Find three things that begin with /s/, like *sun.*

▲ Point to these pictures and say the words: *table, soap, fork.* Do they begin the same? What about *salt, socks, silverware?*

★ Which words rhyme? socks/clocks? Sam/Sally? Sue/you?

♥ What sounds might you hear in a school lunchroom?

READING STREET ONLINE
BIG QUESTION VIDEO
www.ReadingStreet.com

Common Core State Standards

Literature 3. With prompting and support, identify characters, settings, and major events in a story.

Comprehension

Envision It!

Literary Elements

READING STREET ONLINE
ENVISION IT! ANIMATIONS
www.ReadingStreet.com

Characters

Setting

Plot

35

Common Core State Standards
Foundational Skills 3.a. Demonstrate basic knowledge of one-to-one letter-sound correspondences by producing the primary or many of the most frequent sounds for each consonant.
Also Foundational Skills 2.d., 3.c.

Ss

salamander

READING STREET ONLINE
ALPHABET CARDS
www.ReadingStreet.com

Phonics

⟲ Initial *Ss*

Words I Can Blend

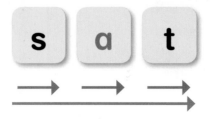

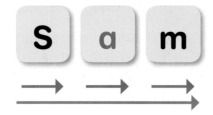

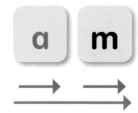

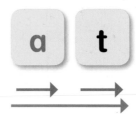

Words I Can Read

have

is

Sentences I Can Read

1. I have Sam.
2. Sam is little.
3. Sam is a .

Common Core State Standards
Foundational Skills 4. Read emergent-reader texts with purpose and understanding.
Also Foundational Skills 3.a., 3.c.

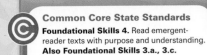

I Can Read!

Decodable Reader

- Consonant *Ss*
  Sam
  sat

- High-Frequency Words
  I
  am
  have
  a
  the
  is

▲ Read the story.

Sam and Tam

Written by Paul Thomas
Illustrated by Katie Snell

Decodable Reader 8

I am Sam.

I have a mat.

Sam sat at the mat.

I am Tam.

Tam is at the mat.

Tam sat at the mat.

Tam sat.
Sam sat.

Common Core State Standards

Informational Text 1. With prompting and support, ask and answer questions about key details in a text. **Also Informational Text 2.**

Envision It! | Retell

NATURE SPY
written by SHELLEY ROTNER and KEN KREISLER
photographs by SHELLEY ROTNER

Big Book

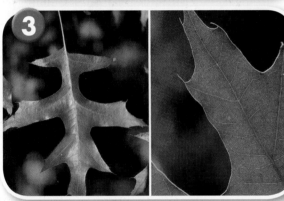

Think, Talk, and Write

1. What did you learn about nature from the story?

Text to Self

2. Where does *Nature Spy* take place?

Setting

3. Look back and write.

Let's Learn It!

Vocabulary

- Talk about the pictures.
- What grows near your home?

Listening and Speaking

- Follow AlphaBuddy's directions.
- Act like an animal.

Nature Words

flower

tree

leaf

grass

Listen for Directions

Be a good listener!

49

Let's Practice It!

Fairy Tale

- ● Listen to the fairy tale.

- ■ How can you tell this is a fairy tale?

- ▲ Why does the elf grant Josef three wishes?

- ★ How do Josef and Anna waste two wishes?

- ♥ Tell why you think people like to read and listen to fairy tales.

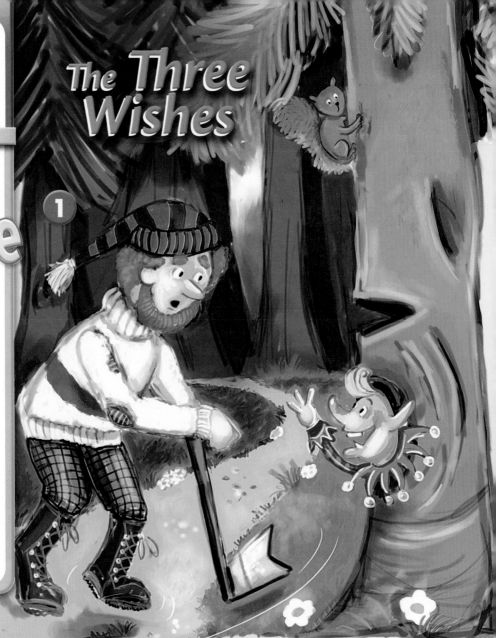

The Three Wishes

Common Core State Standards

Foundational Skills 2.d. Isolate and pronounce the initial, medial vowel, and final sounds (phonemes) in three-phoneme (consonant-vowel-consonant, or CVC) words. **Also Foundational Skills 2.b., 2.e.**

Let's Listen for

Initial Sounds

Read Together

● Say *Pat, Pam, Pete.* What sound do you hear at the beginning of these names?

■ Find three things in the picture that begin like *Pat.*

▲ Point to these pictures and say the words: *paper, panda, penguin.* Do they begin the same? What about *pig, door, street*?

★ Name a color you see in the picture. Clap the word parts. How many claps?

READING STREET ONLINE
BIG QUESTION VIDEO
www.ReadingStreet.com

Common Core State Standards
Informational Text 2. With prompting and support, identify the main topic and retell key details of a text.

Comprehension

Envision It!

Main Idea

**READING STREET ONLINE
ENVISION IT! ANIMATIONS**
www.ReadingStreet.com

School

Common Core State Standards
Foundational Skills 2.d. Isolate and pronounce the initial, medial vowel, and final sounds (phonemes) in three-phoneme (consonant-vowel-consonant, or CVC) words. **Also Foundational Skills 3.a., 3.c.**

Envision It! | Sounds to Know

Pp

penguin

READING STREET ONLINE
ALPHABET CARDS
www.ReadingStreet.com

Phonics

Initial and Final *Pp*

Words I Can Blend

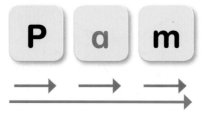

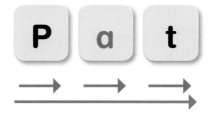

Words I Can Read

we

my

like

Sentences I Can Read

1. We have a map.

2. We like the map.

3. My map is little.

Common Core State Standards
Foundational Skills 4. Read emergent-reader texts with purpose and understanding.
Also Foundational Skills 3.a., 3.c.

Phonics

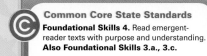

I Can Read!

Decodable Reader

- Consonant *Pp*
  Pam
  map
  tap
  pat

- High-Frequency Words
  I   am
  have   a
  the   my
  we   like

▲ Read the story.

READING STREET ONLINE
DECODABLE eREADERS
www.ReadingStreet.com

My Map

Written by Jerry Moore
Illustrated by Chris Brown

Decodable Reader 9

I am Pam.

I have a map.

The map sat at the mat.

I tap my map.

We tap the map.

We pat at the map.

We like the map.

Common Core State Standards

Informational Text 2. With prompting and support, identify the main topic and retell key details of a text. **Also Informational Text 1.**

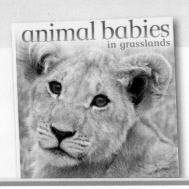

Big Book

Envision It! Retell

1

2

3

4

5

6

Think, Talk, and Write

1. How are most animal babies the same? <small>Text to World</small>

2. What is *Animal Babies in Grasslands* about?

 Main Idea

3. Look back and write.

Common Core State Standards
Speaking/Listening 1.b. Continue a conversation through multiple exchanges.
Also Language 6.

Let's Learn It!

Vocabulary

- Talk about the pictures.
- Where do these animal babies live?

Listening and Speaking

- Say one thing about yourself.
- Listen to others talk about themselves.
- ▲ Retell facts about a friend.

Words for Animal Babies

puppy

kitten

chick

calf

Discussion

Be a good speaker!

69

Common Core State Standards
Literature 1. With prompting and support, ask and answer questions about key details in a text. **Also Literature 2., 3., 5.**

Anansi's Hat Shaking Dance

Let's Practice It!

Folk Tale

- ● Listen to the folk tale.

- ■ Where and when does the story take place?

- ▲ Why does Anansi put his hat back on?

- ★ Tell about Anansi. What is he like?

- ♥ Share ideas about what you learn from Anansi that can help you.

- ✳ What questions do you have about this folk tale?

Common Core State Standards
Foundational Skills 2.d. Isolate and pronounce the initial, medial vowel, and final sounds (phonemes) in three-phoneme (consonant-vowel-consonant, or CVC) words. **Also Foundational Skills 2.b.**

Let's Listen for

Read Together

Initial Sounds

- Say *Carl, Cam, Cate.* What sound do you hear at the beginning of these names?

- Point to the cart in the picture. Find three things that begin with /k/, like *cart.*

- Name other words that begin with /k/.

- Point to and say, *Carrots and cucumbers are in the cart.* What sound do you hear repeated?

- Say *cucumber.* Clap the word parts. How many claps?

READING STREET ONLINE
BIG QUESTION VIDEO
www.ReadingStreet.com

Common Core State Standards
Literature 5. Recognize common types of texts (e.g., storybooks, poems).

Comprehension

Envision It!

Realism and Fantasy

READING STREET ONLINE
ENVISION IT! ANIMATIONS
www.ReadingStreet.com

Common Core State Standards
Foundational Skills 3.a. Demonstrate basic knowledge of one-to-one letter-sound correspondences by producing the primary or many of the most frequent sounds for each consonant.
Also Foundational Skills 3.c., 3.d.

Envision It! | **Sounds to Know**

Cc

cactus

READING STREET ONLINE
ALPHABET CARDS
www.ReadingStreet.com

Phonics

Initial and Final Cc

Words I Can Blend

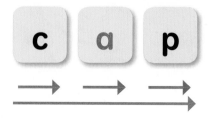

c a p

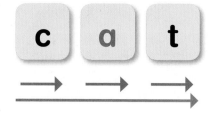

c a t

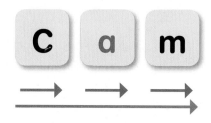

C a m

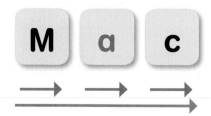

M a c

Words I Can Read

we

my

like

Sentences I Can Read

1. I like Cam.
2. We like to sit.
3. We like my cat.

Common Core State Standards
Foundational Skills 4. Read emergent-reader texts with purpose and understanding.
Also Foundational Skills 3.a., 3.c.

Phonics

I Can Read!

Decodable Reader

- ● Consonant Cc
  Cam
  Mac
  cap

- ■ High-Frequency Words

I	am
we	have
a	is
the	my
like	

- ▲ Read the story.

My Cap

Written by Sue Bear
Illustrated by Lori Burk

Decodable Reader 10

I am Cam.
I am Mac.

We have a cap.

Cam is at the cap.

Is the cap my cap?

Mac is at the cap.

Is the cap my cap?

I like my cap.

Common Core State Standards
Literature 1. With prompting and support, ask and answer questions about key details in a text. **Also Literature 2.**

Bear Snores On   **Big Book**

Envision It! | Retell

Think, Talk, and Write

1. What does a bear do in the winter? Text to World

2. Which story is about real animals? Which is about make-believe animals?

Realism and Fantasy

3. Look back and write.

Common Core State Standards

Literature 3. With prompting and support, identify characters, settings, and major events in a story. **Also Speaking/Listening 2., Language 6.**

Let's
Learn
It!

Vocabulary

- Talk about the pictures.
- Which season is your favorite?

Listening and Speaking

- Where do AlphaBuddy's stories take place?

Vocabulary

Words for Nature

spring

summer

fall

winter

Listen for Setting

Be a good listener!

Rock-a-Bye, Baby

Let's Practice It!

Lullaby

- Listen to the lullaby.
- Sing the lullaby. Sway in time to its rhythm.
- Which words in the lullaby rhyme?
- Who is often a main character in a lullaby? Why?
- Which part of the lullaby is make-believe?

Common Core State Standards
Foundational Skills 2.b. Count, pronounce, blend, and segment syllables in spoken words. **Also Foundational Skills 2.**

Phonemic Awareness

Let's Listen for

Initial Sounds

Read Together

- Say *Isabel, Izzy, Inga.* What sound do you hear at the beginning of these names?

- Find three things that begin with /i/, like *Isabel.*

- Point to these pictures: *ink, iguana, igloo.* Do they begin the same? What about *insects, books, posters?*

- Say *inventor.* Clap the word parts. How many claps?

- What sounds would you hear in a library? What kind of voice should you use?

READING STREET ONLINE
BIG QUESTION VIDEO
www.ReadingStreet.com

Comprehension

Envision It!

Sequence

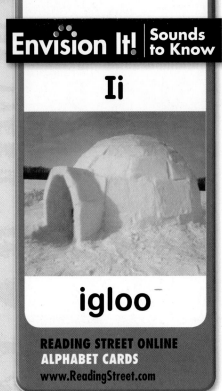

Envision It! | Sounds to Know

Ii

igloo

READING STREET ONLINE
ALPHABET CARDS
www.ReadingStreet.com

Phonics

🔊 Short *Ii*

Words I Can Blend

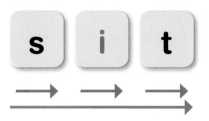

s i t

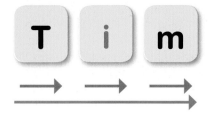

T i m

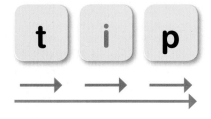

t i p

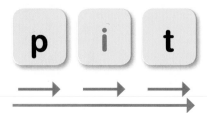

p i t

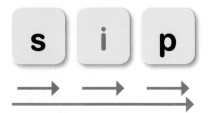

s i p

Words I Can Read

he

for

Sentences I Can Read

1. He is a cat.

2. The cat is for Tim.

3. He can sit for Tim.

Common Core State Standards
Foundational Skills 4. Read emergent-reader texts with purpose and understanding.
Also Foundational Skills 3., 3.a., 3.c.

Phonics

I Can Read!

Decodable Reader

- Short *i*
  Tip
  it
  sit

- High-Frequency Words
  is
  a
  he
  my
  for

▲ Read the story.

READING STREET ONLINE
DECODABLE eREADERS
www.ReadingStreet.com

Tip and Pat

Written by Kate Brand
Illustrated by Carl Johnson

Decodable Reader 11

Tip is a cat.

He is my cat.

Pat is a cat.

He is my cat.

It is for Tip.

It is for Pat.

Sit, Tip, sit.
Sit, Pat, sit.

Envision It! | Retell

A bed for the winter

Big Book

1

2

3

4

5

6

Think, Talk, and Write

1. Which bed reminded you of *Bear Snores On?* Text to Text

2. Where does the dormouse go first in the story? Where does she go last?

↻ **Sequence**

3. Look back and write.

Common Core State Standards

Speaking/Listening 4. Describe familiar people, places, things, and events and, with prompting and support, provide additional detail. **Also Language 6.**

Let's Learn It!

Vocabulary

- Talk about the pictures.
- What do you do to get ready for school? Use sequence words.

Listening and Speaking

- What do the clocks look like?
- What do the dogs look like?

Vocabulary

Sequence Words

first

second

next

last

Give a Description

Be a good speaker!

Common Core State Standards
Literature 1. With prompting and support, ask and answer questions about key details in a text. **Also Literature 5.**

The House That Jack Built

Let's Practice It!

Nursery Rhyme

- ● Listen to the rhyme.

- ■ Recite the rhyme. Clap your hands to show the beats.

- ▲ How does Jack feel about his house? How can you tell?

- ★ Tell about a time when it rained on you. Did you feel like these animals felt?

2

3

Common Core State Standards
Foundational Skills 2.d. Isolate and pronounce the initial, medial vowel, and final sounds (phonemes) in three-phoneme (consonant-vowel-consonant, or CVC) words.

Phonemic Awareness

Let's Listen for

Initial Sounds

Read Together

● Say the sound you hear at the beginning of *in, ask, sign, pears, cast.*

■ Point to the picture of *in.* Find a picture that begins with /i/, with /a/, with /s/, with /p/, with /k/.

▲ Name other words that begin with /i/, /a/, /s/, /p/, /k/.

READING STREET ONLINE
BIG QUESTION VIDEO
www.ReadingStreet.com

Common Core State Standards
Literature 5. Recognize common types of texts (e.g., storybooks, poems).

Comprehension

Envision It!

Realism and Fantasy

READING STREET ONLINE
ENVISION IT! ANIMATIONS
www.ReadingStreet.com

Envision It! | Sounds to Know

Ii

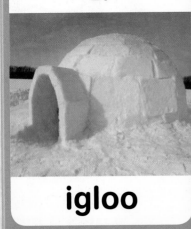

igloo

READING STREET ONLINE
ALPHABET CARDS
www.ReadingStreet.com

Phonics

Short *Ii*

Words I Can Blend

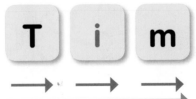

T i m

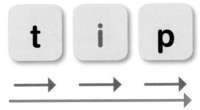

t i p

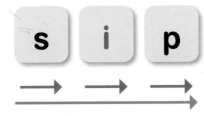

s i p

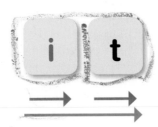

i t

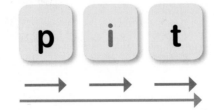

p i t

Words I Can Read

he

for

Sentences I Can Read

1. He is my cat, Pip.
2. Pip can sit for Tim.
3. He can tap it.

Common Core State Standards
Foundational Skills 4. Read emergent-reader texts with purpose and understanding.
Also Foundational Skills 2.d., 3., 3.c.

I Can Read!

Decodable Reader

- Short *i*
  sit
  Tim
  tip
  it

- High-Frequency Words
I	am
have	he
is	my
we	a
for	

▲ Read the story.

Decodable Reader 12

Tim and Sam

Written by Joei Shavitz
Illustrated by Lawrence Paul

I am Sam.
I sit.

Tim sat.
I have Tim.

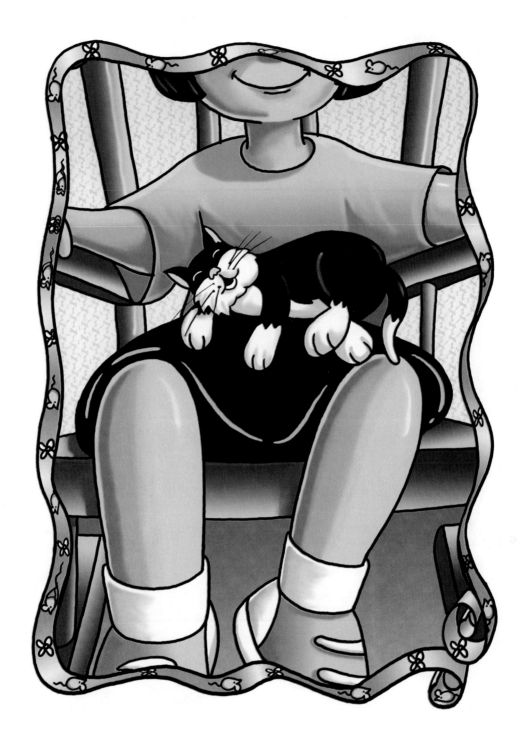

He is my cat.

I pat Tim.

We tip.

I am Sam.
I sit.

It is a mat for Tim.

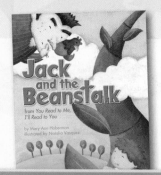

Big Book

Envision It! | Retell

READING STREET ONLINE
STORY SORT
www.ReadingStreet.com

Think, Talk, and Write

1. How are the plants in *Flowers* and *Jack and the Beanstalk* the same? How are they different? **Text to Text**

2. Which story is real?

Which is make-believe?

Realism and Fantasy

3. Look back and write.

Common Core State Standards

Literature 3. With prompting and support, identify characters, settings, and major events in a story. **Also Language 6.**

Let's Learn It!

Vocabulary

- Talk about the picture.
- ■ Raise your right hand.
- ▲ Raise your left hand.

Listening and Speaking

- What happens in the story?

Vocabulary

Direction Words

left   right

Listen for Plot

Be a good listener!

Let's Practice It!

Expository Text

- Look at the title and the pictures. What will the selection be about?

- Listen to the selection.

- How do roots help a plant?

- Where are the leaves on a plant?

- What does the author tell about first? second? third? last?

Parts of a Plant

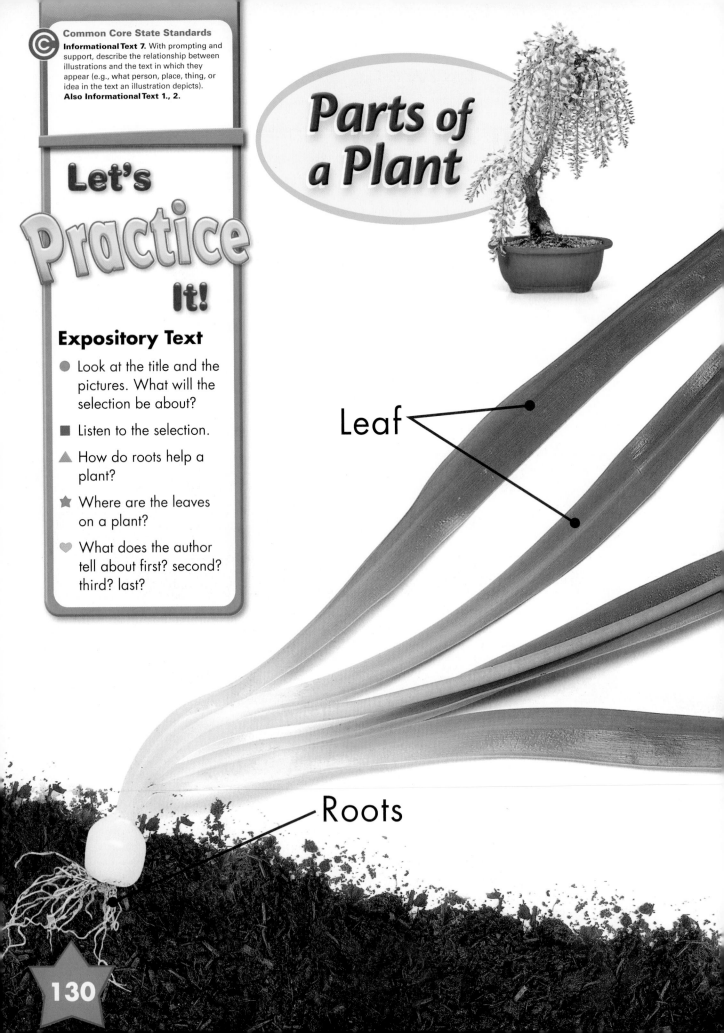

Leaf

Roots

Flower

Stem

Words for Things That Go

airplane

bike

truck

car

bus

van

boat

train

Words for Colors

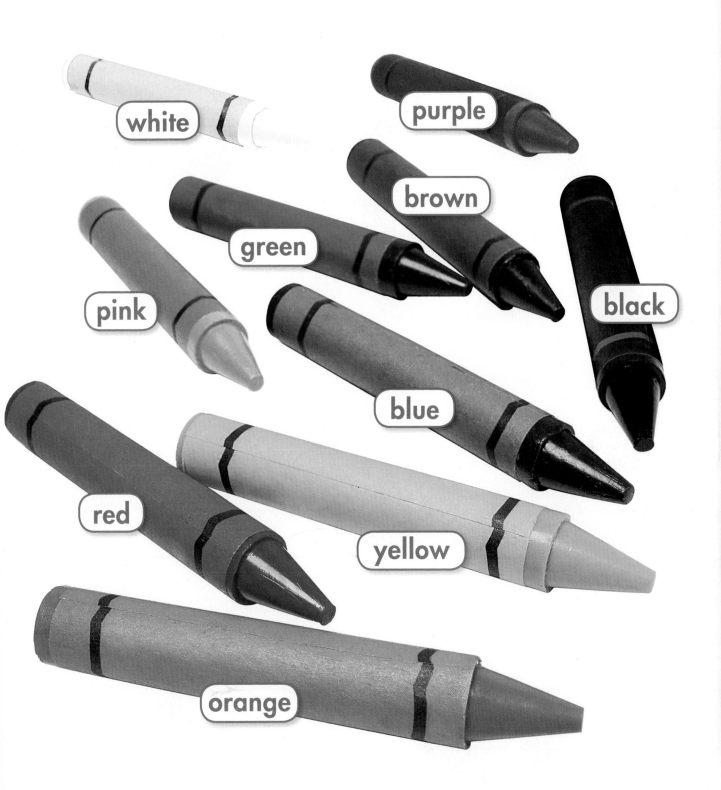

white

purple

brown

green

pink

black

blue

red

yellow

orange

Words for Shapes

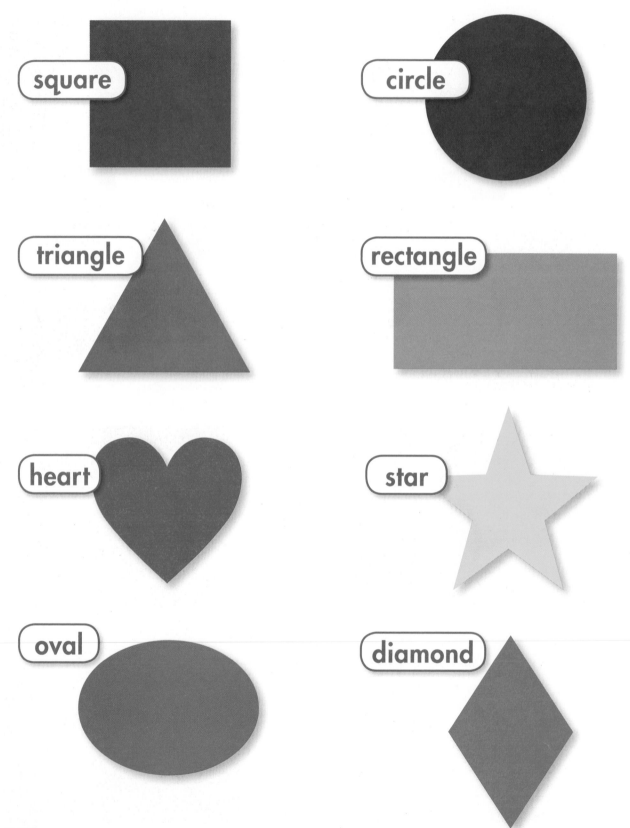

square

circle

triangle

rectangle

heart

star

oval

diamond

Words for Places

school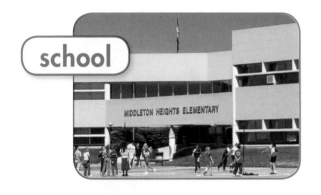

home

park

train station

police station

fire station

post office

library

Words for Animals

lion

mouse

puppy

dog

cat

kitten

duck

turtle

chick

hen

rooster

bird

butterfly

fish

whale

caterpillar

bear

panda

beaver

calf

cow

Words for Actions

skip

walk

run

fly

swim

ride

jump

hop

138

Position Words

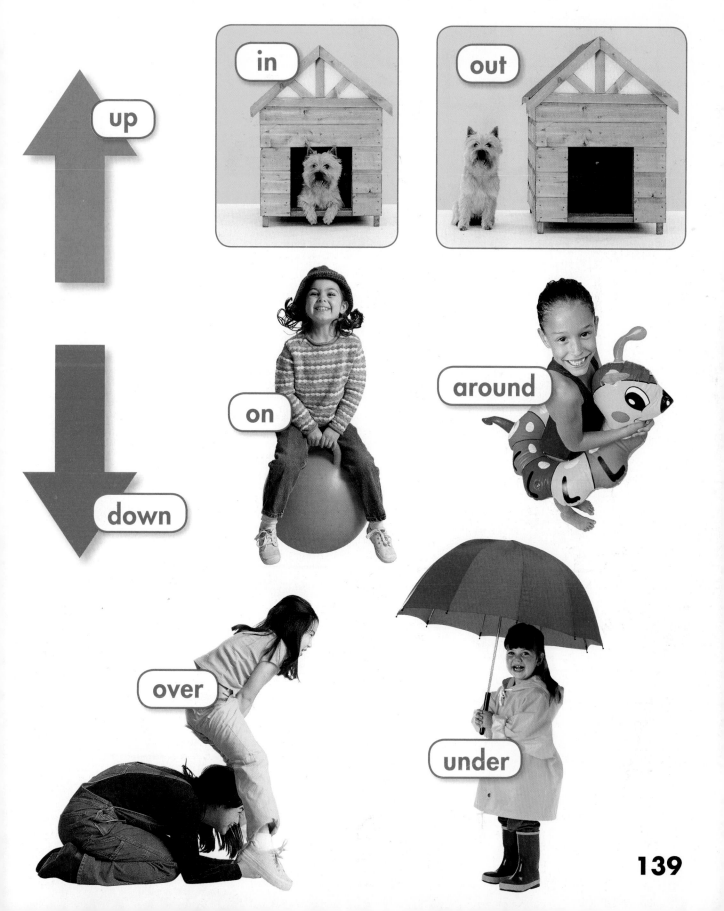

up

in

out

on

around

down

over

under

My Classroom

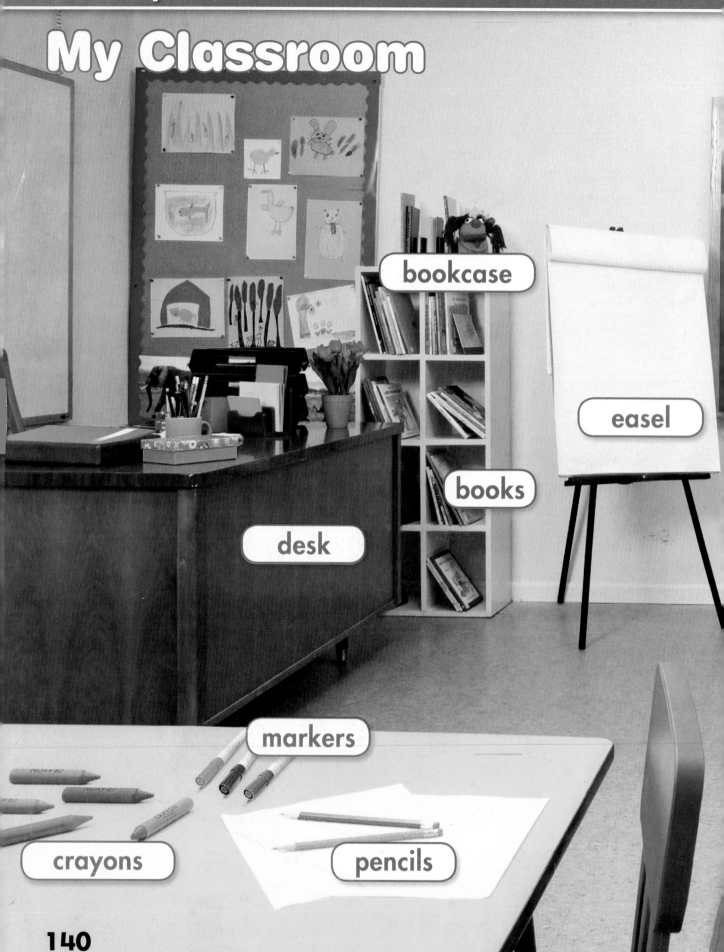

bookcase

easel

books

desk

markers

crayons

pencils

teacher

toys

paper

chair

blocks

table

rug

Words for Feelings

happy

frightened

worried

excited

angry

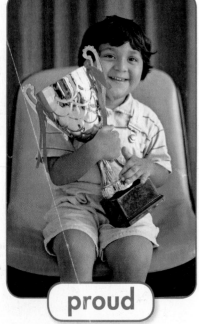

proud

sad

surprised

My Family

mom
mother

dad
father

sister

grandmother

grandfather

brother

8–109 Mick Reid

n

rias

y Kirwan

stin Clar

ewis

Atkinson

my Simard

Ho

Robbie Short

Photographs

Photo locators denoted as follows: Top (T), Center (C), Bottom (B), Left (L), Right (R), Background (Bkgd)

10 (B) ©William Leaman/Alamy

16 GRIN/NASA

36 ©Sozaijiten/Savvas Learning Company

49 Cyril Laubscher/©DK Images, Dave King/©DK Images, Geoff Brightling/©DK Images, Mike Dunning/©DK Images

56 (TL) ©Jan Martin Will/Shutterstock

68 ©DK Images, Jane Burton/©DK Images

76 ©JLV Image Works/Fotolia

96 ©mario beauregard/Fotolia

116 ©mario beauregard/Fotolia

130 (T) ©DK Images

131 (T, B) ©DK Images

132 (CR) ©Basement Stock/Alamy, (TR, TL, TC, BL) Getty Images

133 (B) Getty Images

135 (BCL) ©Guillen Photography/Alamy Images, (BCR) ©Kinn Deacon/Alamy Images, (BR) Flavio Beltran/Shutterstock, (TCR) Photos to Go/Photolibrary

136 (BR) ©Arthur Morris/Corbis, (CC) ©Cyril Laubscher/DK Images, (TL) ©Dave King/DK Images, (BC) ©Gordon Clayton/DK Images, (CR) ©Karl Shone/DK Images, (CL) ©Marc Henrie/DK Images, (TR) DK Images, (TC, BCL) Getty Images, (BL) Jane Burton/(c)DK Images

137 (CR) ©A. Ramey/PhotoEdit, ©Comstock Images/Jupiter Images, (CL) ©Cyndy Black/Robert Harding World Imagery, (CC) ©Dave King/DK Images, (BR, BC) ©Gordon Clayton/DK Images, ©Rudi Von Briel/PhotoEdit, (TC, BL) Getty Images

138 (TR) ©Rubberball Productions, (BR) Jupiter Images, (TL) Photodisc/Thinkstock/Getty Images, (BC) Photos to Go/Photolibrary, (TC) Steve Shott/©DK Images

139 (TR, TC) ©Max Oppenheim/Getty Images, (CR, BR) Getty Images, (C, BL) Rubberball Productions

142 (CR) ©pete pahham/Fotolia, (BL) ©Simon Marcus/Corbis, (TR, TL) Getty Images, (TC) Jupiter Images, (C) Photos to Go/Photolibrary, (BR) Rubberball Productions